Pink Sunset Luminaries
Collected Poems

Pink Sunset Luminaries
Collected Poems

© 2018 by Marie Marchand
Fine Itinerant Press
www.mishiepoet.com

Marchand, Marie, 1972 –
Pink Sunset Luminaries Collected Poems
Library of Congress Control Number: 2018911069
ISBN: 9780692192733

First Edition
Printed in the United States

Author Photo: Steve Van Ausdall

To My Son & Husband

Dryw —

May your creative voice emerge

as sustenance for a life full

of beauty, compassion, and hope.

Your value as a human being

is immeasurable. I love you.

Steve —

An old and new light in my life,

you helped inspire this book into being

by believing in the power of creativity

and the necessity of poetry in life.

Thank you.

Table of Contents

I. LOVE

you whisper Amen
weight of your breath in my palm
art of love beheld

What You Say

These words,
strung together
with a delicate touch,
emerge from
your throat
  charmed, peerless.

Shrouded in a mysterious etymology
they move with the centripetal force
of mercury, all blood pulsing
  to gather in the heart.

Like syrup they flow
into my empty places
  filling me. ◆

Wyoming

I have to see what this is
I have to go to it
explore, wonder
impose myself
split open the dustcloud and dry land
bring my rain

I have to touch this untouchable
listen, receive
sit under the big cedar sky
and wait

wait to see
how the past reemerges
in time ◆

Love's Threshold

How some people pilgrimage
to their holy sites
    is how I come to you.

At your sacred threshold
in the fragrant wood,
I set an intention:
May my inner convolutions untangle and heal
so I may know the manifold
    truths of you.

Could it be you were made for me?
That from the beginning
these hands were fashioned
to cradle your heart?
Tenderly, as if it is a
    newborn sleeping.

Yes! I believe yes.
So with ginger steps
and quiet humility,
your heart within me,
I walk into a future illuminated
    by love.

My movements upon the loamy earth
release wafts of honeysuckle
encircling me like a halo—
nature's sign that beauty
   has awakened.

A sign that everything about
you and me
   is right. ◆

What About Love

Love is not a transaction
but a transcendence.

Love is not a selfishness
but a radiance
ineffable and wide.

Love is not a ladder
but an already there.

Love is not a slog
but an ahh.

Love is not a recipe for confusion
but a bright clarity.

Love is not a bed of nails in an icy cavern
but a long sought-after shelter
that calls the heart its home. ◆

Songbirds

for Steve on the occasion of our wedding

my love for you is bursting
with a thousand crystal
beams of light
then fusing into the one
luminescent mystery
I behold today

you are my heaven
my truest of true loves
an opulent angel surrounding me
with tenderness and grace
a weightless wonder
of halos dancing
glowing a crescent moon

your beauty is a fountain
whose source is as plentiful
as the boughs of hydrangea
I carry through your harvest field
blessed by sun and sparrow's call
taste of clover in the wind
a meadowlark's dream
to sing as brightly as this

as sweet as a songbird
is how I breathe you in ✦

Proposal

From here
is enough
he said
on bended knee
basking
he said
in me

From here
inferring before here
time lost
but let's not think
about that

From here
inferring now
into forever
time enough
when love exists beyond
the bounds of
memory

From here
in your heart bathing
means forever
after and before
since the beginning
love a circle
you catch me
and all my falls

from yesterday
are erased
your net spreads farther than time
we collide and exist
as one
our futures
and histories enmeshed

From here
now
an eternal wonder
she said yes
and it became the truth ◆

Heaven on Earth

When do we come down from heaven?
That mellowful plain of dreams
where you love me whole
as if I came from you.
How else could it be
my happiness, my fate.

In you heaven is omnipresent
kneeling inside our
hallowed place
our inheritance.
It will never drift unbeknownst
into the locking folds
of memory
for it will never cease.

Heaven is Aristotle's
perfect contemplation
the indivisible mover
celestial inward sky.
Heaven is our love.
Love is our heaven. ◆

The Beginning

You once shimmered
in the sun for me.
Your voice so soft
I had to lean in
to hear the
premonition
of your love. ◆

The Meadowlark and Sparrow

I spent years wanting to die.
Too painful,
this life
of tumbling boulders
ravens mad.

It started out differently
in sweet-prickled air
with Meadowlarks
on a prairie sweeping up
to peach hills.
Dainty-legged Sparrows pranced
on my windowsill.
"Good Morning! Good Morning!"
they chirped in bright cheer.
Such easeful awakenings!

I remember the most peculiar details.
Cartwheels, tank tops
bonfires
searching for Penny the lamb.
We never found the woolly pet
among the corn where we looked;
we were too young
to make the connection to
the Miller's supper table.

As an adult I wanted so badly to return
to those days of bare feet on misty grass
and dusty trails.

I willed it in my mind.
I could even taste
the fresh-tended green beans.
Could even smell
the Colorado evening,
its orange perfume
dry grass bloom.

I remember the most peculiar details.
There was a closet
within a closet
twice as dark
where I would retreat when sullen or scared.
I thought no one would find me there.
I was wrong.

I wanted a canopy bed
like my best friend's:
yellow and white checkered.
She was pure.

I remember the most peculiar details.
Playing Old Maid in Pam's trailer
pretending to kiss James Bond
tying flyaway tents in the summer
digging snow forts in the winter—
winters that used to be called emergencies
before Global Warming.
Now the snowstorms are mild, I hear.
Nothing like the glacial silence of
white fields draped.
My reverie.

I remember the most peculiar details
the rest a blur.
Only the things special to me
made it to the surface
of my explicit memory;
they survived
they make me good.
Still, they make me good.

The implicit memory
lives elsewhere buried
a darkness I never want to see
a formless horror
that dilates my fear and intrudes on my life
from its secret closet within.

I spent years wanting to die.
Too painful,
this life
of tumbling boulders
ravens mad.

For years I hadn't seen
the shape of Future
the shape of Hope.
What about now?
What has time sculpted
from my persistence through pain?

Now I have found you;
I am yours.
Now I want to be loved by you
for many thousands of days.
My life is more than half done.
I am closer to my death
than during those years of
pining for a peaceful grace.
Even so, even half done,
the riches that await us
are ever so lusciously free
from human conceptions of time.
Love is the point
no matter when it arrives.
Love is the point.

It is my anointing.
You are my reward.

I have returned
to cool grass between my toes
the sun a prism in the pool;
to the Meadowlark and Sparrow.
Now yours is the song
I want to awaken to. Forever.
Now, with my whole self
I desire to live
through your song
your love
your vision for a future
I never thought possible. ◆

Today's Word is India

The doctor who saved
my son's life
was from India.

It was a snowy day.
Denver, Colorado.
All of us
chilled to the bone.

Once the nebulizer started
I sat down and tried to breathe peace
into my frazzled mind.

I, too, had lost my breath.

After he attended to my son
with a reassuring grin
the young doctor sat down
beside me.

In a melodic harmony
he explained the
anatomy of an asthma attack,
patting my elbow warmly
to calm my nerves.

My breath slowed
but my cheeks were still flush
from the cold.

His dark autumnal eyes,
with lashes long as spider legs,
danced under artificial light.
In them shown
such empathy
as if he were
the father of this child.

His shiny cinnamon skin
and redeeming smile
personified a textbook
bedside manner.

He had found right livelihood.

Did he care about
each of his patients
to this noble degree,
or was he simply
and suddenly
    in love
    with me? ◆

yin yang

a vacant heart
has nothing to give
no fountain to drink from
its reservoir full
of brick

an abundant heart
has everything to give
a spring without depletion
its well full
of love ◆

II. MEMORY

days of stunning youth
distill to word and prayer
poems remember

Favorite Memory
for Pam Miller

In Colorado
dusk lasts forever–
apricot clementine fire
luscious grape divine,
distinct outlines muted
drenched in warm light.

In other words...
    heaven.

For hours after supper
we'd twirl cartwheels
on Pam's lawn until
we could no longer see
only feel
our movements.

Then inevitably
my Mom would yell:
"Marie, Marie! Time to come home!"
And I'd think:
    But I am home, Mom.
    Beneath the sky, tippy toes on the Earth.
    Here, I am.

There I was.
My lithe body tricking gravity
    laughing
    being free.

I did know then
what I know now:
    those times
     were the kernel of life. ◆

Crop Duster

I used to race the crop duster
in golden fields
on dirt roads.
Almost won on two occasions
when his engine sputtered
and stopped midair
the plane suddenly adrift
serene like a silent glider.
Not even the evacuation
of dirty oil made noise
only my footfalls
as I took cover
under the Cottonwoods
evading the downpour by inches
my white summer dress spared.

In general, it seemed good exercise
a brief respite from my
rigorous summer schedule of
sleeping in, cartwheel contests
syrupy lemonade and
crunchy green beans snatched
from the untamed roadside vines.

My best friend and I napped in our tent
a sheet knotted to the strongest branch
of our favorite Weeping Willow tree.
Unsecured corners fluttered in a breeze
scented by fresh watered garden
strawberry remnants.

We dreamed of becoming elementary school teachers
enjoyed the feel of papers in our hands
passing them out to pretend children
with whom we would get stern
only so we could show mercy later on.

When the lazy din of the
cranky biplane woke me up
I'd part the eaves of the tent
and jump out excitedly
full velocity as if
the Messiah
were at hand and I would be
the honored first to see.

No one ever told me to run in the
opposite direction of the plane.
Never warned me not to inhale.
No one knew better then (our excuse).
Looking back, I should have
taken shelter
in Pam Miller's bulkhead
and played Old Maid until the dust settled.

Instead I danced in the July snow
raced full throttle in Paradise Acres
Loveland, Colorado.
Gleefully I chased with mouth agape
the slow-falling candy prisms.

Early on the pilot would laugh at me.
Flash his low-flying smile
speed up and slow down
according to the ambition of my gallop.
A real race I fancied.
I could see the pattern of his teeth
and the way he parted his hair.
He flew that low.

He was my friend.
At least it seemed
until the wind changed.

Five summers into our playful duel
I could no longer muster
enough air to run even
half the length of cornfield.
As I grew older and slower
he showed less and less affection for the race
as if he had grown tired of me.
(Though he too was getting older.)
He would pass me no problem
as my feet jogged clumsily along
my heart feeling as if it would erupt
lungs burning with every sip of crystalline air.
I was no longer a challenge
for the man simply doing his job.
His exuberant countenance gave way to
the occasional rigid salute
given just before he would pull up
and serpentine
through his poison vapor trail.

By the time I turned eleven
he had forgotten me altogether.
Never acknowledged me.
Flying low overhead
he would simply open his shutters
let scatter the ashes
and disappear
into the pregnant thundercloud
leaving me behind
to pant and heave
bent over my knees
until the rattle settled
and the burning went away. ◆

FIERCE

creative
full of struggle
verging on the manic & mad
i have lived a full beautiful life
regretting only one thing
not kissing you
for if i had,
that kiss
would be there
for me to remember it
but because i didn't
all i have to remember
is my longing for you
which goes on
and on ◆

Letter to Superman

for Christopher

I was six years old when I saw
the movie Superman.
My mind, in its natural child state,
could not reconcile the difference
between actor and character.
Weren't we just watching other
people's lives, only magnified?
Isn't this what life will be like
when I get a job and fall in love?

At that moment, Superman replaced
Elvis as Man of My Dreams.

That night I wrote Superman a letter
inviting him to spaghetti dinner at my house.
"What should I write on the envelope, Dad?"
"Just Superman, Honey. He's so famous
his mail doesn't need an address."

Dad assured me Superman would get my letter.

Regrettably Superman never showed.
Crestfallen, I could not come to terms with it.
As an adult I have entertained
the archetypal Superman:
This one sitting across from me must be him.
Or this one lying beside me
or the one opening the door for me
so gentlemanly.

As a girl I did not understand that
Clark Kent and Superman were the same person.
Clark Kent isn't my type.
It's not that I am opposed to vulnerability,
only to weakness.
Vulnerability can be sexy, whereas weakness
connotes an unwillingness to live courageously.
Unforgivable in my eyes.
Alas we are not perfect, can never be perfect.
But we can be brave in our imperfection.

I am a woman now, not a girl
a writer of many love letters scented
kept under the pillows of men
in a lovelorn diaspora.
Flowery philosophy, passion
and lyrical assemblage
of words caught between pages.
Stories of the heart catalogued.
These do not die as love dies:
They stick to memory.
It takes 100 years for paper
to crumble or melt to the touch.

My childhood linguistic
is lost to memory.
Forty years later
the only words I recollect are:
handsome, love, spaghetti.
Still I imagine my letter to Superman
to be the most tender piece
in my archive of prose.
It expressed
my belief in a
promise to be fulfilled,
my trust that love will win out
no matter how fictitious,
my notion that it is never too late
to be innocent again. ✦

Resistance

Around the dinner table
worlds either bloom or collide
flourish or implode
oppressive banter
forced speechlessness
quiets a soul

Around the dinner table
9, 10 years old
expression squelched
"Shut up," "Shut up" the refrain
followed by stern shouting
alienating my will

Around the dinner table
to interject anything
even "pass the butter"
was impossible
making my corn on the cob
a brittle bone

Around the dinner table
now my own cherry oak
I mend, most of me, slowly
not verbose oh still terse
but fear gone
intimidated no longer

Around the dinner table
I remember how that
sauna of silence
filled my lungs with
deafening cement
I somehow learned
to exhale

Around my dinner table
I try to listen
allow love
I contemplate release from prison
and the miracle
of vitality ◆

Invisible

This missing
is inconsolable.
It follows me,
waiting for the
moment when
I am alone.
It comes then
to rattle and disturb
what is left of me.
When my shadow
leaves that moment
to engage the world,
people talk to it
thinking it is me,
though I am still
in the memory
of your holding. ◆

Lost

I used to be intrepid.

I look at old photos of myself smiling
and I say, "Who is that?"

Day by day my hallowed light shrinks
as if I've swallowed the key
to my own destiny and am being
kept prisoner from my true self.

People who have lost themselves are like ghosts
and there is no right door to walk through. ◆

Elvis Coffee Table Book

At a time when other little girls my age
cradled Cabbage Patch Kids
I carried my Elvis coffee table book
    wherever I went.
My Mother couldn't have pried
that book from my sore arms
even if she'd tried
with all her might
I held on so tight.
Me and Elvis. Elvis and me.
    Inseparable.
Skinny or fat, did not matter.
Loved him all the same.
Any.
  Way.
   He.
    Was.
Dead not quite one year.
Tragic.

Wherever I went
Elvis went too:
    to school (first grade)
    to the grocery store and mall
every random place
for easy access
so that at any time I wanted
I could look down and steal a glance
    at his handsomeness
    and be comforted by how familiar he had become to me.

As young and demure as I was
in little yellow barrettes
I wasn't immune to idolatry.
I wanted to understand his life:
    the climactic timeline of it
      his desires and aversions.

He was just like us in that regard
Buddha might muse:
    Disquiet, rambling mind
    loneliness
putting his pants on
one leg at a time
    as they say.

My sacred fidelity
was how I memorialized
the man who bought every
police officer in my Dad's precinct
a brand-new Cadillac.
New York, New York.

While the other kids
took naps on their
carpet squares
    I stayed awake
    with my eyes closed
      dreaming of Elvis
not knowing that one day
life would take it out of me
    just as it did him. ◆

In Spirit & In Flesh

to recollect the evanescent quality
of our communion
in spirit and in flesh
how passionate we were
   even before we knew love
   and melted into one
how my arms and entire body would tingle
and I had no problem giving things up
to be with you like this

remembering the sensation
like I was walking slowly through a cloud
the weight of my body enveloped by the buoyancy
of my deepest sensualities unleashed
no gravity to hold me down
and believing that at any moment
I could evaporate
and be taken back into God
leaving behind my hold onto
this world with such remarkable ease
   no sorrows, no regrets
for in that space of tingling, weightless body
when we were perched upon rocks
and dolphins leapt over us in joy
   I LIVED FULLY.

guided by indiscriminate passion for life
a wound of longing was opened and constant
a longing to reexperience union
with the one true source of Love.
I gleaned the beginning in your eyes
and there was no question that life was good. ◆

Morning Light

Your chestnut hair grazes my belly, chest.
In my memory, my dreams.

Memories arise when I smell macadamia nut coffee.
I used to stir the flavor into coffee beans.
It was my job at Morning Light.
The other girls wore gloves
but I liked the feel of my hands
swirling around in the jar.

A meditation of sorts.

My skin absorbed the caffeine.
The ambrosial scent ran up my arms.
My senses were heightened
sympathetic response activated
   when you walked in
   when you sat down
   and were beautiful.

When will you write to me? ◆

Timeless
for Annette

She said, "Everything is temporary."
Through her tears
I heard a mournful mantra
meant to conjure all the things
she'd ever lost.

It made me think of blessings
and how people always say
to live in the present moment
because we cannot change
the past and do not know
the future.

People equate imagination
with the future: we imagine
castles, love and quietude.

Especially peace.

Imagination resides in memory
too; swirling around within
that which appears to be
fixed in time.
Those elusive belongings we
spend our lives catching
and holding and losing.

These memories are not the domain
of yesterday but are everpresent.

This is our fruit, our sweet consolation
our hope that nudges our hearts
to expand in the light.
It is not temporary:
it lasts forever
even beyond our bodies.

We can rest in this sacred knowing
that all things go back to God
and infuse the universe.
All things become timeless.

Especially love. ◆

III. TRANSCENDENCE

half-moon awakens
pink sunset luminaries
burnt peach scent of night

How to Become Human

seek serenity
accept benevolence
allow transformation

a bowed head
receives grace

the body becomes
a tunnel to
amnesty and light ◆

Sense

I can sense the propinquity of your body
by the sound of your peculiar foot-stepping
over fallen autumn leaves, a rather swift gait
rustling and cracking
wind and fire

I can sense the intense closeness of your body
by the way you maneuver through the
stealth choreography of topiary gardens—
a menagerie of hearts gone wild
your favorite kind of petting zoo

It is not long before I sense your entrance
onto this ephemeral stage
and it is not long before
you start dashing behind lions, pigeons,
long-stemmed sweetheart roses—
odd items of bramble that shape
themselves in stagnant play under the
nimble tutelage of a shy gardener's shears

It is not long before you begin swooning
amidst poppies not long before you expire
a sleek desert wind through fissures
in the bodies of statues

With an air of quaint anonymity
you shift in and out of my field of view
dodging soft corners pretending to
blend into the backdrop of greenery
and landscape fooling only yourself
while the effulgence of your soul
wildly dawns
blinding my eyes from this
garden path of stone

In the mirror of the darkness of the night
when subdued in gentle repose
from the stark agency of day
I visualize the imaginal way in which
we are drawn into one another
I fancy the quick measure of
hiding and seeking between
formal re-introductions
and downward glances that fall
into the safe neutrality of floorboards—
quite an awkward dance we perform
yet it continues to shape the contours
of our souls' deep longing for return

I chase you bare-chested
and shimmering beneath the
cool shoulder of a twilight moon
whispering after your name
in the clutch of a pressing night
I long to birth any and all configurations
of life inseminated by the pivotal
blueness of your deep soul

In consideration of our proximity both
physically and in terms of the psyche
and all that we have to lose
it is no wonder we are so
utterly drenched in delirium

Slipping away in shivers
swinging the gate of the garden
I silently mouth desirous liturgies
gone astray from the mind of God
and it is no wonder we are so
utterly drenched in delirium

Composing concertos for guitar and orchestra
conceiving a pedagogy of love and risk
waiting for the birth of this child ◆

The Drafted Stream

Returning to the fields
to lay down
one last time
in the soft beauty
that once held me.
My fall this time
will be felt inside
the land unendingly.
Here where it meets
the sky on the horizon
capturing me between.
I am born here
so naturally
here released.

The feathering wheat
lifts its face to the
strange and
final quiet
taking me along
in its silent
wind-drawn wake.

Before the jarring snap
my broken listless sigh
I hear kind words
spoken over
a lifetime.
A compendium of
language and love
I leave behind
except slivers of
the most sweet
I take to the open
unknown peace.

I sleep in the glinted barrel
give in to the drafted stream.

With a graceful spin
diaphanous white
my dancer body drops
conforming to the
cradle of the land.

A blanket over
my eyes
the wheat's caress
will be
a stunning release
into finality. ◆

Olam

Olam is the world
the place where God hides
the place of shifting
colors and tides
where ecstatic forms
beg me to seek and
to seek exhaustively
and then to give in
go to sleep
go to sleep
and I do finally give in
finally exhale
embraced by this lofty day
engaged in warm breath
of remembrance
against the mountain
this mountain
such a bold piece of earth
how it reeks
of the insidious relations of passion
that, lingering, do not give up
how it reeks of the whispers of our history
full of beauty
full of the sense of infinitude
but very past
very unknown to these present days

We used to search the secret places
the interior body of the mountain
used to swim in the moonlit bogs
feigning death
through drowning
out of breath
waiting for the other
to find us
and drink us
down into the river of the soul
never to be found again
never to want anything again
as we had wanted one another here
in this clandestine valley
where, as mystics,
we scoured the sand, the wood,
and the faces of the other
in search of God

Olam is the world
the place where God hides
where God plays within the distance
an outstretched arm allows
the distance of an outstretched arm
away from our folly and sin
have we breathed God in
at various times
we have given birth to God
in our souls
from out of my womb
came the life and love of God

Yet even hiding moments away
God is oftentimes sorely invisible
to our parched and blinded eyes
how desperately we seek God's love
how we long for transformation
in the furnace of God's heart
Seeking eternal life, we fall
in love with one another
in the hope of redeeming
ourselves and the world
we fall in love with one another
in the hope of living this life fully
we fall in love in the hope
of rediscovering our true,
essential selves

Behold, the baby's cry
the intertwining love of creatures
the mountain that reeks of our passions
Behold, God is near
disguised in the pallor
of mundane life
but near nonetheless
is God
embodied and free
within Olam
is the world
the place where God hides ◆

Lamentation in Bellingham

This interminable rain
  drowns the spirit.
Any internal sun
remaining is
  doused by oceans
    cascading from the sky.

Even the consoling trees
are over-drenched,
  sitting in puddles
    of God's tears. ◆

Amazement

Your child burns in me
Beautiful, yet unknown
Full of grace, though unseen
Imagined whole, yet unformed

Triumphant new life
Comes through war

Life's resilience
Amazes me ◆

Majesty

for Jacob and Drew

Lost on the high mountain
love is stronger than the storm
filled and surrounded
by memories to keep them warm.
Whiteness a crystal fountain
in water they will be born.

Through fields of white led astray
a mournful sight
to behold this day.
A new path discovered in the light!
Be filled with love as you lay
and sleep peaceably in the night.

Those captured in the cold
become free
into cosmic energy they enfold.
They become the stars we see
their stories forever told.
Now our sweet guides they will be. ◆

Magenta Sky

Cresting over the pink-orange horizon
My shoulders sunned and bare
My woman's body curved
Blazing in passion bearing
As deep as my bones
This sense of you pains me
It pulls me in and swallows.

I lean daringly out over
The edge of myself glowing
In magenta hue fancifully
Imagining your movement
Toward me shimmying closer
And closer.

I wonder:

Would you ever for a moment
Give your soul to me in one
Transcendental fantabulous
Moment when all conceived
Realities fall away and leave
Us simply cleaved swelling
In the unnamed present
As if in a dream?

Our cheeks would be rosied
From dancing fandango.
Our hearts freed in a billion
Points of light diffused unto
The universe smiling.

My mind falls into my heart.
I see angels fly in myriad colors
Dazzling bright.

I see you and me
Immaculately interfused
In this one moment
Poised to last forever. ◆

What If

What if it's not about
      our struggles,
but the kindness
         of others? ◆

IV. BEAUTY

fresh from bathwater
flowery nightgown billows
green apple honey

The Woman

Is she not but an
orthograde manifestation
of any beauty hidden in the
forest, beneath the rock, deep
in shell, wonder of the heart?

She studies with gentle presence
the eddies astir in our heads
our blood rivers
hurricanes.

The man will continue
to go to her to sift
his sins through her hair
deflate his soul unto her chest
and quiet his longings
in the rapture of her soul.

How beautiful, how
maddening it is
to be a woman. ◆

Where to Look

At certain lulls,
sadness slips through
the multitudinous fissures
in our honed personas.
And when we say a word,
it sounds like doves flying.
No one can understand the meaning
beyond the rustling.
Traces of beauty. Trust. ◆

Beheld

He speaks of pomegranates
his fondness for apricots
and me
in the same sentence.
It is true
I cannot imagine
any sweeter company
but what does this mean?

Into the wind garden
we travel this day
blown to a dance
amid chimes
unknowing
trepident
the timbre of voices
unremembered
yet hanging still
in the gale
soft-frayed from
prayers released
a thousand-fold
into the distant
flow of chador
and chrysalis
beyond our cities
of birth.

I remember every part of you.
Your profile in amber light
downwardly drawn
pensive
in wonderment
demure hiddenness
crestfallenness
a tender succulence
to behold.

I adore you.

Into the rain garden
we now step
truant
unrepentant
holiness beckons
refreshment
to delight
our ravaged bones
bemuse our
grappling selves
ready for peace
trembling at present
striving towards
gravitas or merriment
or both.

Whatever we can pull
back into ourselves
will be. ✦

Touch

Her collarbone.
Its shape and milky rose hue
he would die for,
has died for.
He is on his second life now.

Her camisole strap refuses
to stay put
slipping down along
her shoulder again and again.

With a keen eye he watches.

His lissome fingers reach
for her in unstilted mesmery
and though his hands shake
only slightly,
a tremor rumbles inside of her
like a 6.0 magnitude quake.

The ridges of his throat
are mute with awe.
Strands of his hair fall
across his eyes like a
weeping willow in the
yellow light of dusk.

And this is okay because
to see her in her fullness
unobscured
would cause pain somehow.
Pain with consequences
he cannot fathom
for her beauty verges on the sacred,
is sacred.
Something very different to him.
Never before…

This is it.
Silence. Trepidation. Love.
Not even a breath separating them.
Finally she leans forward into him,
his touch a tranquil spider. ◆

Reminiscence a Day Later
for Seva

A contemplative morning
on the last day
wrapped in Seva's arms.
On the veranda
I looked at light
through the trees,
my senseful mind
sifting through crisp birdsong
and the highway's
calming purr.

Can I remember
through this competing din
the horses painted
wild on the plain?

Seva and I met him
at Cheyenne Frontier Days,
the artist who painted horses
starting in swaths of purple
(he never uses black he told me as I cried).

The painting drew me in
caught me thunderstruck,
the canvas thirsty-bright
like the sun cradling the land.

Bold strands of purple
the color of royalty
captured quiet zeal in motion.
Hooves through tall grass
manes swept loose
alive in the abstract landscape
born from the artist's eye
now breathing outside his dream
living beyond his sight
living inside of me.

The wind.
It was about the horses
and the wind
in Wyoming—
how free they are
but only in tandem.

One without the other—
horses without wind
wind without horses,
would be mild and tame.
Together they run and flow
gallop and whirl
in all their magnificent
wildness.

I'd never seen horses
as beautiful as
those on the artist's plain.
Their brilliance brought to me
the soft nuzzle
of a horse's nostrils
felt in cupped hands,
mingling with the image of art
alive in my memory.

Walking through the gallery
with my new lover,
my heart was open
and wild and free.
Wrapped in his love
I was seeing everything
I had never seen before. ◆

Beauty in Chaos

He tried to find
beauty in the chaos
of my mind.
He says he found it.
I believe him.
Usually. ◆

Evidence of the Miraculous

Miracles don't carry with them
signed papers specifying the
time, date or mechanics of
this or that manifestation
of the miraculous.

Rather, miracles move about
in sheerness and stealth as
portals through which God
fulfills His desire to be near us.

As emissaries of God
they are charged with protecting
the inherent mystery
for without mystery
there can be no faith.
If we know everything,
there is nothing left to seek
and seeking is an essential
expression of our humanity.
To seek in faith within
the cloud of unknowing
is our genesis and teleology
our existential premise.

Miracles are hard to figure, however.
Their paradoxical psyche throws us off.
By nature they are hidden, clandestine.
Yet they are born for notoriety
wanting fiercely to be known.

Jesus sent healed people away saying,
"Go and tell no one."
But the glory of God must be
revealed by God's people.
Our telling is revelation
our testimony
evidence of the miraculous.

Miracles rarely shout obnoxiously
or cause a scene in public.
Rather, they emerge
to clothe us in gentleness
douse us with comforting Spirit.
They lead us through locked doors.

Miracles announce themselves
in dichotomous identity as
timid tsunamis of grace
fantastical reminders of God's
perfect unending love for us.
They smile and beam in secret
generating quiet sighs of
awesome gratitude
awesome wonder. ◆

The Broken Lily Lies

Walking in the brisk English air outside your window,
I feel the caress of your eyes against my neck, my legs.
You take keen pleasure in the way I move past you.
I walk knowing you watch me, knowing
You write about my long dark hair
Lifting up into the wind.

> *I met a lady in the meads,*
> *Full beautiful—a faery's child;*
> *Her hair was long, her foot was light,*
> *And her eyes were wild.*

It has happened this way for a year—
You watch me walk;
I feel you watching, but do not look up.
It is 1822 and matters of love take much time.
Yet time is not something we have much of.

Today is the day when I stop beneath your windowsill.
When finally I decide to raise my head to you.
And, as if you knew it was to be the day,
You turn to me immediately and
Flash your brazen, blue-eyed stare.

But this day is too late for us.
Whatever occurs in this longed for
Rendezvous will be time-limited.
It is the eve of your departure to Rome.
In the morning you will leave me wishing
For what had never been.

Then what handsome man, what sensuous poet
Will wait at his window the full length of day
Simply to see me pass?
Like the still unravished bride
Upon your Grecian Urn, I will remain
Untouched by you, John Keats,
And have only your words

To enfold unto my breast.
I will mournfully recount your
Every delicate poem and ode,
Your bold epic tales,
And gently bespoken letters of
Exhaustive love penned in a fury for me.
Take me with you! I cry in vain.

You may say there is too much we do not know;
So much we guess at.
And yes, on a certain level, we are strangers.
You do not know my last name- my father's name.
Nor do you know of my work, age, or the books I like.
Yet I am unafraid.
What superfluous matters are these!

Perhaps you guess that I have read your poetry
In the prominent journals. You may hope that
I haven't read the unjust, malevolent criticisms
Hurled at you in those same journals.
(You will bring these to your death,
Afraid of 'sinking into nothingness.'
Tragically, in life, you will never know how famed
Your remembrance will be – Beyond your ever imagining!)

Perhaps you suspect that,
Just as you watch me walk,
I watch you write.
Though you have no idea
Of how I come to your window at midnight
To witness your silhouette arranging
Words in motion with insomniatic zeal.
I feel these words on my body as you write them.
Every letter brands itself in burnt rhythm against me.
I suspect their emergent form to be more sensual
And triumphant than your hands would be;
More so than in the moment when your body
Would come near me, ecstatically.

>*Catch the white-handed nymphs in shady places,*
>*To woo sweet kisses from averted faces,-*
>*Play with their fingers, touch their shoulders white*
>*Into a pretty shrinking with a bite*
>*As hard as lips can make it*

This is why you watch me walk.
This is why you write about my hair,
My gait and glance, the color of my eyes
Through the iced window pane.
I am the woman who worships your words.
I am she who feels them as potently as you.

Do you still say there is so much you do not know?
O, there is so much you do!
You know I have passion for life;
That I desire to have this passion
Fulfilled through your body in mine.
You know the likeness of my soul.
What else is there to know but this?

"Beauty is truth, truth beauty,"- that is all
Ye know on earth, and all ye need to know.

So take me with you. Take me!
I know you are going to Rome to die,
Just as you know it, as you knew with
Your mother and sweet brother Tom.
Though you have wooed death's coming
On wings of the Nightingale,
You are not ready to be taken alone.

Do not worry for me. I am prepared, my love.
Perhaps more so than you.
I will cradle your head in my lap,
Run my hand against your cheek
In the hour of your death.

I see a lily on thy brow
With anguish moist and fever dew,
And on thy cheeks a fading rose
Fast withereth too—

Why would you deny me this? You are a poet!
How could you not understand that to feel
The fever of your last breath against the
Hairs of my forearm, I would give my soul?
You will be as defenseless and helpless as an infant.
My love for you can be a monument to your final
happiness. Let me be this for you!
Let me kiss your lips as they grow cold.

One kiss brings honey-dew from buried days.

Otherwise, my young poet of only twenty-six,
You will die never having known my sweet embrace.
You will have missed life's flowering-
The very goal of which is joy.

Let me be your solace in God's Light,
To heal o'er you – your skin's sweet balm
To the meadow of moon and midnight calm
While to my chest I hold you tight.
Alas! Pale eyes uplift, uplift!
Into the Sterling Bright
Your soul must drift.

And this is why I sojourn here
Alone and palely loitering;
Though sedge is withered from the Lake
And no birds sing— ◆

Italicized lines from John Keats. Title borrowed from Percy Bysshe
Shelley's poem Adonais: An Elegy on the Death of John Keats.

V. WONDER

dragonflies crisscross
nighttime garden rapture light
heaven grows wild

Diffraction

You cause light to bend simply
                 by rising from a chair.
             It follows you in
         waves, encircles you.
A halo of changed
    light, charged light.
      It shines on me day and night
          warming my chilled Northwest bones. ◆

Remember

for Dryw

Sometimes hope is
a wild Chihuahua
hidden in a cave
hunkered down all
cozy-like out of
sight yet ready to
bark its little head
off to protect you. ◆

to do ◆
to do or not
and we must choose
"doing" he just does
need not contemplate the
one difference is the beaver

skill
his unerring
his fortitude
in his ingenuity
offspring human-like
lodge for his mate and
to construct a suitable
human-like in his ambitions

home
making a
animal is
the coarse brown
looting leaves and mud
as adhesive glue and gum
hoarding scraps branches bark
Building placing stacking pasting

beaver
building

Sweet Hesitance

I did not give it but a second
of time
in that lilting moment
before looking down and
turning my chin away.
A wave of shyness overcame me then
and locked my lips so that all I could think to do
was whisper a muted goodnight.

He stepped back and the moment
that could have been was gone
like a breath expired
something half-forgotten
though still historical
still significant.

The moment now a memory never known.
An imaginary kiss foreign to our lips. ◆

Dream of the Balloons
for Arica

She has her mind fixed on Albuquerque.

It's her dream to stroll beneath
the fire-breathing bellows—
colorful birds as big
as behemoths
imposing their lightning souls
upon an orange-kissed land.

A multitude of joyful dragons
in limitless sizes and shapes:
SpongeBob
Darth Vader
Princess Leia (RIP)
her side buns shimmering.

Vintage stripes and wavy lines
diamonds dwarfing people
busy on the desert floor
directing pilots
charting plumes of smoke
this moment up til now.

State flags, checkers, peace doves
solid pink and tiger's eyes
all these hopes and fantasies
silhouetted
against the cloudless sky.

Albuquerque.
She goes there every year
in her mind.

This vision captured by
her imagination
is just about as clear as
the real thing could be.

Someday, however…
Someday she will fly. ◆

Song in the Desert

Shadow of the Cross
moves along the desert floor
blood-colored dust
henna in sweat
tawny symbols
upon skin
    imprint of sages

Steeple, center of the land,
grants a shady refuge
to wayward, forlorn hearts
martyrs wandering the wilderness
threshold of thirst
    speechlessness
            awe

baby blue sky about to bloom
    Hello Santa Fe!
        Sing
            to
                me ◆

The Essential Question When It Comes to Healing

when an implicit memory
of darkness
the kind that pervades your life
is buried

is it best
to let it lie on a bed of whispers

or coax it to the surface
with candied enticements (on a good day)
or boiling rages (when it's bad)?

the essential question we face:
does it have to be seen to be healed?
does it have to be seen to be healed?

or can we send light into it anonymously
fill it with warm honey
and kiss it goodnight?

then, I imagine
the monster's power will be usurped by the light
then, I imagine
you will finally have Peace,
the elusive dove that's been encircling you
your whole life, but never entering

now, she will ◆

One Beautiful Thing

One thing God has taught me:
It is never too late
to be innocent (again) ◆

Dear Emily

Not the thing that flutters in the trees,
Hope is a wild Chihuahua hidden in the caves.
It is not an aspiration we can measure
And take steps to achieve,
But some elusive thing
That skirts our field of view
Purposely, cruelly as if a game.
Some say hope is bright like angels' wings
Though no one knows for sure.
It lives behind a mask
We break fingernails
Trying to pull off...
Any coarse action to shed its light
Upon our mad eyes.
With these eyes that peer lonesomely
Like neglected children into a void,
We see our pre-baptized selves
Through a glass darkly.

All we want to see is
The true, enlightened hope
And to be fed by it
If only for a moment
If only for a moment. ◆

The Possibility

Seems like being kind
has gotten me nowhere.
My alacrity falls to
the ground thin as smoke.
The bitter cinders fly
unnoticed in the wind.

Not that I am necessarily expecting
a quid pro quo with the world.
I will be kind regardless.
Yet I have to believe
it will return to me
someday.

Theologian Paul Tillich wrote:
Vitality resists despair.
I ooze vitality.
I beam.
Yet my despair persists
and my vision of surrender
draws near.

Will my strength hold up?
Will I fold like a ghost
into the unforgiving cyclone?
Or will the truest of true loves
come sweep me off my feet
and shower me with kindness?

I have to believe. ◆

VI. SPIRIT

behold communion
sheer reverence becoming
the body a church

Follower

Unguided, unmoored
I did not learn about
God early on.
There was no time
or space in the chaos.

Instead, God learned about me.
How to insert the Spirit
into my frenzy
and distress.
God followed me
through wildernesses
manic geographics
my whirlwind attempts at life.

God came to terms with
my off-kilter nature.
God said: "Ok. This is what
she is doing. This is how
she is. I better go along
for the ride so
I can be seen by her.

Did you know God can be
so accommodating
in her fierce and loving desire
to be seen by us? ◆

Dispersion of Good

There is no right path in life.
No single destiny.
The will of God is not exclusive,
but manifold.
The will of God is Love.
And Love, the creative energy of the universe,
has assorted openings for grace.
It invites.

When Love is our destiny,
everything is possible.
Every place we find ourselves
is where we are meant
to be. ◆

Stillpoint

I am giving up chaos for Lent.

Instead of giving in
to confusion and pain,
I choose to feast on
pardon and peace.
Pardon because I am good enough
to be set free from my mistakes.
Peace because I need a still mind
to heal my daily severance
from God.

Chaos takes a toll.
It disorients the mind,
makes the body tremble
in hypervigilance.
It drains love of life
from the heart.

For forty days, I give my chaos to God,
the one with a knack for transmuting it
into gleaming dust of the Universe.

A perfect order from disarray.

Through this consecration,
chaos reconstitutes into light
and good things
are made
from my disordered life. ◆

Most Beautiful Gift

new eyes see the world
carried and held in spirit
glimmer of angel
you were a baby
in my arms
just yesterday
how did 17 years
go by?

in my dream
Jesus held you out to me
you were a heavy, furry cat
in his arms
he gently rolled you over
and revealed your under belly
with fresh stitches
and tender skin

he touched the wound gently
and some blood seeped out
when I recoiled
and implored him
not to touch again
he held you out to me and said:
"Oh no. Don't worry.
He'll be okay." ◆

Narrow Mercies
or Scars as Signs of Life

Once a saber hit my face
spinning really fast.
It broke my nose
cut open the skin
struck a quarter of an inch
from my left eyeball.
A quarter of an inch from
blindness and disfiguration.
I walked out somber over
the stitches and the scar.

When I reminisce about it now
I realize something magnificent:
God has been following me around
this whole entire time
averting tragedies
by a quarter of an inch
letting me slip narrowly
on either side of danger
nudging me casually
redirecting flawlessly
time and time again
from blindness into light.

Each of my scars another life
that would have gone unlived
had it been any other god
altering my movements
by a slight breath
the weight of a strand of hair
delaying a sneeze here, tilting
my head a few degrees there.
I dare people to mess with me.
Bring it on Fire, Lions, Spinning Metal
People With Nothing to Lose.
Stitches disintegrate into the body.
I absorb fear and nothing clings to me. ♦

Revealing Light

Coughing fits
Alleluia
still alive
every breath a signal
of a battle won

Every breath a gift
they say
even amid struggle
if we persevere
there is Love
in pockets shining forth

Love blooms from struggle
It is our redemption
our reward
It is Creation
the Divine within

Coughing fits
Alleluia
every breath
a gift

Every breath
a sacred vow
to go on
go on
go on

No matter the cost
love is the way
If we open
our frozen hearts
we will be healed ◆

The Ministry of Being

A thousand birds
sing out
celebrate
the new day
pale mist orange dawn

A thousand prayers
rise up, disperse
the dusky currents
of water and wind
our daily bread

A thousand desires
slough off
cast away
the false self
its chains asunder

A thousand breaths
quiver in peace
the new self
renewed in Christ
emerging for you ◆

Daughter

Daughter whose faith made you well
Who Jesus sent away in peace
You forced your way through a
Pressing crowd to touch merely the
Hem of his clothing
Knowing that you would be healed
Through this simple act
And your bleeding stopped.

Your faith pulled power from Jesus
And he noticed this for he called you forth
So that he could see the person with
Such abiding faith.

Daughter of faith give light to the
Small seeds of faith within me.
Help them to grow into trees
That will shade this world
Burning from the fires of
Nuclear intention and
Waywardness from God.

Teach me Daughter of Faith
To never leave go my reaching
For the fringe of God's cloak. ◆

and then...

and then she sat in prayer
giving everything to God
because her little earthly body
could no longer contain
the depth of suffering
she encountered in the world

prayer broke her fall
when nothing else could

it captured her in its net
and rocked her
like it was a hammock
in the summer breeze

then she became porous to the wind
that blessed her with good things
such as abundant hope
and vibrant imaginings

God shifted her locus of control
tightening her circle of concern
just a bit
not enough to harden her heart
or dilute her compassion
but just enough
so she could live outside
the fortress of grief
she'd been captive in for so long

just enough so she could breathe
in the open air
and feel hope for the future

her giving everything to God
was like a boomerang except
everything that came back to her
was good ◆

Shelter in the Desert

How do I explain belief
when its salient feature
is mystery
translucent
bare?
While mystery seems a negative knowing
a fill in the blank
it is not an absence
but a presence.
It is. I AM.

It exists both as a psalm taking shape
and completed verse
setting the context for life
the frame for meaning
from the beginning
preparing the milieu for reflection
on what can and cannot be.
How do we release the dreams
we've held for others past their time?
When they've given up
we've never let go.
Hold on, or release?
Shall we dance?

Mystery is a weighty substance
invisible yet perceived
in the sanctity of silence
a ghost upon the skin.
Mystery surrounds us
like heat in the New Mexico desert:
unseen, yet palpable.
Something greater than ourselves
young souls who are lost yet blooming still
somehow
through belief.

How do I explain belief?
Knowing we are loved frees up space
so we can hold infinite love for
an infinite number of people
for the Earth
and for God—
the ultimate Mystery. ◆

Seeking Solace After Letting Rozie Go

after it was done
after her small last breath
I wrote to him:
    There was life
    I signed a paper
    There was death

He wrote back:
    There was suffering
    You signed a paper
    There was peace ◆

VII. PERSPECTIVE

aspen leaves tremble
curtains lift in summer wind
sun moves through small cracks

Trust

Walking into a room
the air billows
in a silent wake rippling
like doves' wings
or wind on a pond

We are constantly
creating effect
never truly still
From our first suckle and cry
we shift energy
simply by the
expansion
of our lungs
For better or worse
we are connected
by the strand of God

We hope for our actions
to be loving
at least innocuous
and for the results
to be fruitful
But somewhere
down the line
someone is hurt
sometimes even when
our offering is
an aching smile
or olive branch

To always be generating
consequences
along our timid sojourn
is a painful inheritance
a tiresome endeavor

It doesn't mean
we are bad people
It just is humanity
The Second Noble Truth
contends our attachments
cause this wake
from the get-go
Extinguishing conditions
may take lifetimes
Yet it is possible
to be free

Fold the poems, honey
Slip them in an envelope
Mail them to the universe
and trust ◆

Prayer in the Desert

'Be still' says the wind
hazy and dry
tasting of sage.
'Seek serenity' prods
the light on the river.

In this spare landscape
certain things find
themselves closing,
others in bloom. ◆

Day After Mania

open eyes, open
to the blue world
stay awake to look
around and see

what you did yesterday
in feverish amusement
drove 50 in a 25
laughed the whole way
spun out of control

10% cautious observer
90% wild, hungry
for sensation
color saturation
speed rain body touch
couldn't get enough of
brash raw elements

10% sighed relief
upon arriving home
90% climbed the roof and
danced atop the skylight
stomping until it cracked
drip, drip, drip

open eyes, open
you are in deep
the ramifications
start now ◆

Cold Spell

In a cold spell
texts are frozen bound
and the mind
caught between the pages
steeps ◆

Now

In one moment
there is just
enough time
to wonder
how long
the moment will last
and then the moment
is gone. ◆

Profundity

My dog is barking
at the mannequin
in the store window.

How can I tell him
she is not alive? ◆

Insanity

How can I
expunge
this eager flare
ever present as of late?
You follow me around
distracting me from business.
I hear your throat echo
as if I am
responding to voices
inside my head.

I invite you
to touch me
so I can move
through you
and be
sane again. ◆

Until

Until I suture myself
people will continue
to fall through me. ◆

Bountiful Measure

Dylan Thomas
clean precise
immutable art
the meaning of life
revealed in masterful
arrangement
sentiment
word play
each objective met
tightly constructed phrases
free of clutter
no extraneous thought
no unnecessary expression
brilliantly taciturn
imagery
syllables
in rhyme or not
dart around corners
one stanza to another
perfection on paper
he operates purposefully
on a sparse lexicon
the outline of branches
no leaves to obscure
brevity
a pithy linguistic
these are his
bountiful measure ◆

VIII. RADIANCE

tendrils of tall grass
aesthetic of synchrony
fall in together

Brightness and Dust

Aloft
in the mystic garden
wet from the river soak
I witness your persona
fading backward
to soft
shedding its
white sleeves
in favor of what
our reverie believes
when you walked
into a coffee shop.

Every memory
piercing the
brightness
we hold inside.
Olden brightness
a sacred tide
untouchable
except by us
washed of sin
the only two who know
the bareness that
cold pulls in.

In your delirium
you speak truths
you may not otherwise.
Your tongue eased by a
wearied
unfettered mind
for which you apologize.

Only I won't take what you say
with a grain of salt
for I love this prose
when from your lips
opening like a rose
it drips.
Through years you sift
to find your essence
in remembrance
your imaginal world
a gift.

This whimsy of word
is my fate
the language I speak
the only verse
I've heard.
It is how I navigate
through the heartache
I curse
and into the beauty
I seek.

A Siren I swim
in the swell
of your waters.
Your words go through me
splendid secrets
you tell.
In the shimmer of moonlight
we are not ready to see
the beauteous reflection
of what could be.

Your words go by:
a river
I can't touch twice
though I try.
Swish my hands in the rushes
to catch them
so quickly they flee.

Ill-fated endeavor of trust!
As if searching
for a single thread
of saffron
after a thousand have
been tilled
into dust. ◆

Carrying the Scent of Montana

chiffon floats
diffuse as pollen
over delicate shoulders
billowing golden hue
Van Gogh's brightest
wheat
self-adoring in speckled
sun
flowing lengths of material
with flowers dyed
clasping a cascade of quiet
air—
one slight exhalation
breathed
on lover's skin a few towns
over
in slow motion
candlelight ◆

Missoula Catalyst

You balance tip toe
    On a narrow shelf
Tucked behind the waterfall
    Soft glare of amber eyes
Ridge of shoulders strong
    Taste of salted water spray
Across your forehead, lips
    What I would give

Preparing to pierce
    The cascade, you linger
Calculate velocity
    Anticipate the angle of slice
Exact degree of tilt
    The sound of water-rush
Opaque, blinding
    Fingers strum the mist
To no avail, you are
    Lost in lightlessness
20 meters skyward
    Poised on a veranda
Set into the steep rockface

You must choose at random
    With hurried recklessness
One stark moment to
    Release your fear and
Fall blind of your bearings
    Into the gleam
Of turquoise below

To get to this spot
    Where you are now
You have devised an
    Entire choreography
To avoid cutting your thigh
    On the sharp sleeve and
Joint of rocks
    Held together by
Force of water centuries-run
    To flatten and caress corners
That jut like knives in time
Evolution's persistent torrent
    Will make this jagged hook
So exquisitely smooth
    Not even a woman's
Silken shoulder
    Will compare to the
Upward sanded sweep

You bite your bottom lip
    Cut it with your teeth
A final deliberation
    Before you muster a
Moment free of fear
    When calculations cease
Arms stretch wide
    Palms up
To gather light azure

Body taut, hollow
    Resonate like a lute,
You tip forward
    Into the rushing sheet of
Cool river milk
    Sheen vapor glazing skin
Dappled now with
    Sunset hues
Smile glamorous
    As a movie star's

After all that nervous lingering
    Blind and tip toe
On the wet stone ledge,
    This drench of surrender
You ride with spontaneous ease
    A silhouette of cloud-fire
About to hit the eddy going 60

Between then and now
    However
This lofting shiver
    Becomes you,
Smile Like the Sun;
    Lips speaking silent words
Taken by the wind
    Unwrote poems drowned
Unknowingly in the place of nevers
    What I would give
To find those words and
    Write them on your arms
Shoulders, hair long
    Sonnets on skin

You will never be more free
    Than you are now
In this moment
    Tremulous, determined
Taste of salted water spray
    On your tongue, lips

What I would give
    What I would give
What I would give ✦

Jewel in His Eye
for Dryw

Dragons, skateboard, Mama
the beautiful boy
lights up the world
says "Yes"
stepping out onto
the porch
tiptoeing to the ledge
of life
looking back at Mama
only once
before dropping in
for real
the 12 ft. wall
VERT
blue eyes smile
fearless dreaming
the jewel in his eye
before he goes
I see it glimmer
my baby boy grows up. ◆

three minutes 32 seconds

the time it takes to
dance
into the mystic
Van Morrison echoing in
the station usually dark
now alight
when the woman asks
the first question she
doesn't want to
and hears the second
best answer
from the gentleman's lips
she misses already
never having known them
but still ◆

Lilac Soul

I breathed rumors of its fragrance
even before the purple bough
was shaken free and cut.
Beauty is effusive.
It travels like dust in a shaft of light
noticeable only in stillness.

Beauty floats, it swirls,
it slides under locked doors
to the other side
going undetected until we rest
then we see.
We are called. Not loudly.
Just a whisper is the invitation
to be free.

What holds us back?
Are we brave enough
to step out of our castles, jails,
porches, fallout shelters
our cocoons, coffins,
our frayed and wearied selves?
And if we manage that, then what?
Will we be brave enough to Dance?

Like Aspen leaves applauding in the sun
caught in the sweep of unbound joy
our old selves put to rest in shadow and ash.
Our hair, clothing, everything will be
scented lilac; we become new (again).

The edge of life is the end of fear
and the beginning of everything good.

The white flag washes over us
like angels' wings.
We are left holding the sunburst.
Empty. Open. Gorgeous in the light. ♦

Lightness and Rock

You stand overlooking the sea
from a high plane on a brazen jetty
facing the chill tempest alone.
You stand among the sharp rocks
and point daringly up to sky
as if you are one of them
as if you exist beyond the extent
to which she created you.

I come to you, to that beyond
I look into you, not through
no one can look through
you are too solid
your bone like heavy rock
only your hair is light
for your soul is heavy too
strong, grounded
though I have balanced it
on stretched fingers.

When I am with you
I touch both lightness and rock.
In raving scarlet and gold,
daybreak's sheer wonder illuminates
the upward crescent of your neck
your sharp cheekbone (just as she described).

Poised on firm rock
you turn to greet me with red hair flaring
against the turquoise backdrop of sea.
Your sterling eyes survey my
body, mind, purpose for living.
Your self-assurance… dazzling.

I stand before you holy diaphanous.
The open collar of my sheer blouse
falling from my shoulder scented
lime verbena and vanilla.

I have never been afraid to be like you.
In moments of exultation
and pure love of existence
I have seen only the ocean, the sky
and your figure before me.
I could never loosen you from my
intellect, character, being.
Like the moon, I absorb your brilliance.
I contain you.

Even though she would never sanction it
and would disregard me with contempt:
I own you, Howard Roark.
I own you.
I never wait for you.

Even though she and you reject the concept
of someone owning someone else
it remains this way.
Her method was not fail-safe.

She created you.
Her golden offertory to the world!
She set you atop a pinnacle of granite
and made you laugh.
I will never give you back. ◆

Incandescent Grace

i. the parts of fire you know

Fire is known in degrees.
You know it better than most.
Few have studied it as you have:
with intensity, precision.
You must know it, or you
would never return from it.
Yes. You know fire.
You are able, in your sleep,
to recite its chain reaction
and point to its constitutive
elements on the periodic table.
You can slide through it
and survive.

Fire has various typologies.
For you, fire is nemesis.
You know things about it
that others do not know:
Its scent prior to the billow of smoke.
The feel of its prickling vapor on skin.
How to calculate its weight and velocity
through populated space
or a wheat field.
Its deftness rounding corners.
How it quivers in sheerness
impairing lines of sight.
Its manner of rising.
Where it congregates.

Its relationship with air.
How it swirls with wind
brightens in light
is doused by tears.
You have learned
to move through fire
without being burned.

ii. the parts of fire you forget

While you consider it deadly,
others crave its radiant heat
to loosen the fright of dark
and keep our babies warm.
Pinecones crackle and open
announcing rebirth hidden in ash.
Burning candles on a window sill
illuminate shiny lovers' skin.
Mystics use the word to describe
union with God.
The poet writes of its symbiosis
with physical desire, artful passion.
Chihuly forges wonder in it,
his hands and arms branded
by the alchemy.
Isadora Duncan dances naked
against its flare of orange gleaming
on the surface of the sea.
This is the arena of intangible fire.
A genre difficult
to move through
unscathed.

iii. heat: fire of the body

Burning deep within
the fury of sense
a quickening skin
a frantic, joyful enterprise.
Though fierce, this type
of fire can be quelled,
pacified in the moment.
Still, true as true fire,
it rages the color of wild birds
(copper, fuchsia, lapis lazuli)
in a flash against cloudless sky.
Its kindling is tenacious.
It will engulf you and
make you new.

iv. oxygen: fire of the heart

While not easily ignited,
the fire that burns in the heart
is impossible to extinguish or subdue.
A gesture of awe awakened,
it scorches the outer shell of
our good, forgotten selves
revealing exquisite fruit
dripping in thaw.
As close as humans come to purity
this type of fire.
Surrender is advised.
There is no use.
No hope of restraint
for the heart is impulsive,
coaxed in irrational directions.
There is no adequate rebuff
to chaos
only a voluntary exhalation
into its strange entanglement.

v. fuel: fire of the soul

Heavy is the human soul.
It does not move adeptly.
Rather, it is the stationary
application
of our deepest, roughest
personality fighting for.
Soul is the petroleum fuse
that ignites instantaneously.
Its combustion ravaging,
not methodical or graceful.
Just mighty.
Forging prose out of thirst
endeavoring risk upon risk,
there is no sense in fighting
this fire, so deep it bellows.
You must go in expecting the heat.
Better to release your held breath
and succumb.
The soul catches a wisp of string
a sheet of amber rushing
a cache of dynamite
centered in the untouched place.
It refuses to wither;
it's just that we have to find it
and find it over and over again.
That is what life is about:
remembering to find our soul.

vi. every beautiful thing

Fire rages tiger-like in myriad places, forms.
Not all that fire touches is destroyed.
It sparks life
soft light
warm breath
a gentle kindling
heart
soul
caught open
in the midst
of flame
a merciful reprieve from the cold.
Michelangelo's ivory light
Van Morrison's edgy drawl
cello
every elegant kiss on her silken arm, shoulder, neck
incandescent grace.
Every beautiful thing
a consequence of fire
bursting open from the soul
nemesis to lover redeemed, if.
You can slide through it
and survive, if.
You are willing to be new
over and over. ◆

Autumn Grace

The comfort of autumn
Sweeps slowly in
Degree by degree,
Sienna to gold.
Vine Maple's red fire.
Blaze of Sweetgum,
Raywood Ash.
The once glorious sky
Seems unexciting now
Compared to these
Lava-bright skeletons.

A dewy chill rides
The morning air
Dressing our glad houses
In sparkling stillness;
An uncanny quiet laid
Full of Earth noises rustling,
Yet peaceful as a lullaby.

With every rush of wind,
Crinkled leaves detach from
Trees ready for retreat.
Umber flakes wrestle downwind
To scramble our hair and
Hide in the loose weave of
Our cozy wool sweaters.
A strange sprinkling of
Found objects
We gather.

Autumn woos us into a
Rustic dormancy with
Scented musk of pine
And chimney smoke.
We are lured by the
Human inclination to
Curl inside ourselves
In an act of
Anonymous surrender
Blanketed by a Charcoal sky.

Walking underneath trees of
Burnt clove, magenta hue
Arcing elegantly
Across city streets
(A seamless bridge
Season to season),
We forsake propriety
In favor of kicking, sprinting
And shuffling noisily through
Piles of gilded fringe,
Blinded by ginger aswirl.
Our stride lengthens
In the coolness as
We breathe away the
Summer heat that has
Collected in our skins.
As evening quickens, our
Reddish glow turns wan;
We are ready for a long,
Turmoil-less drowse.

Held-in close
Under autumn's canopy
Fragile brilliance,
We are reminded that
Everything must be
Let go of
For newness
To begin again.
Every freshness that
Awaits us in springtime
(Joy, passion, giddy mirth)
Moves through fissures in the
Architecture of our psyches,
Detecting vulnerable strata.
Premonitions await genesis
In the hollow space
To germinate unbeknownst
While catapulting our fears
Far enough away so that
We no longer believe them.

But first, under
Cinnamon leaves
We sleep. ◆

Color of Wild

I have never heard his name
after all this time, you'd think
      but no, never
I couldn't even take a guess
or make one up
there is no squeezing someone
      into a mistaken name

while I am ignorant of
      the sound
that signifies him
      the word
that lends him identity
I do know
      something
about him

      I know his eyes
I recall their brightness
      in my sleep

open to the world
eager
      alive
blue as the ocean
reflecting the sky

          Cyan, Lapis Lazuli
three shades brighter than
          Matisse's Blue Nudes
cheerful, phantasmic
like the churning
sun-drenched river
that takes you
          down
          one minute
and settles pristinely
into quiet
          the next

          a shocking hue
reminiscent of
another world
a tropical destination or
South American rainforest
          eyes the color
          of wild
birds and coral reefs
waterfalls I hide behind in my dreams
even cliffs Elvis dived from
          or so we believed

          a shocking hue
well-deep
fresh water bubbling up
a fresh drink
so young
          stark

too young for nostalgia
still memorable
to the before-world
guileless in his
        satisfying
        youth
whereas I am clueless
        about
        his name
I know his eyes like
when today becomes
        yesterday
and I look back
and laugh at all my
        silliness
as if reflected
in a wooded lake

there is no need
        to guess at
the beauty of his eyes
for it is evident
in his sweet
        demeanor
        smile
effervescent perspective
        on things

I wonder
does he see blue
      looking out
as the world does
      looking in?

this type of blue
this chronology of spark
      and glow
rarefied electric
      indeed ◆

IX. BELONGING

soft feathering wheat
bending shivering brightly
bare ankles run through

Curtains

the hover and swoop
of dragonflies
sweet effusion of Lavender

I hear and smell
lying on my mother's bed
it is summer and a breeze

comes through the window
that opens to the Colorado plain
sheer white curtains

flow over me
barely touching me
as if a hint or whisper

requiring stillness
awaiting the next breath
nothing could be as peaceful

as curtains lifting and waving
in and out of half sleep
empty mind I rest

this is what I remember
of my childhood
it will be my last memory

a gift that holds me
even now
sometimes it is the only thing

that reminds me
of who I really am
an innocent girl

housed momentarily
in this wayward stolid form
sometimes it is

the only thing left
after a lifetime of seeking
what is good ◆

Gratitude

this day is a gift
this allotment of time, grace
this amazing breath, wonder
this sunshine, golden beauty
this birdsong, blessing

this is the one day
happening now, right now
the only thing
here
a compilation of moments
making a whole
say yes

breathe in peace
breathe out turmoil, past hurts
breathe in forgiveness of others and yourself
breathe out resentment, fear
reimagine new endings to your trauma
your brain will believe you
and remember
gratitude changes neural pathways
it expands your heart
and extends your life

embrace gratitude
seek acceptance of what is
if only for a moment
let beauty take hold
and you will be free ◆

Poem for Anyone Who Has Ever Struggled to Like Themself

Out of 12 chromatic notes
emerge
infinite variations of
rhythm and resonance.
Songs that sing
homemade lullabies
to the human spirit.

Out of seven billion people
you have emerged.
One unique and
beautiful you!
A song that sings
color and light
to the aching world.

You are an unfinished symphony.
A genius composer, eclectic singer-songwriter
who creates infinite timbres of beauty.
The only person in the world
who can be you.

So be yourself.
And be a good one. ◆

The Effect of Land on the Soul

There is a fallenness to life.
Not an awkward skidding,
or a turning away from angelic fate.
There is that, but not now, here.
This fallenness is a movement
of our bodies and minds shedding,
leaving pieces of ourselves
in ruffled piles at our feet—
crested souls flaking in the wind.

We see memories teetering
wondering where to go
when the container
can no longer hold
the depths and pinnacles of life.
When it seems the joys
are as mighty and cumbersome
as the sorrows and fatigue.

"How is it I can love this much?"
the broken heart asks.
A good broken, full and ripe.
Broken like Communion.
Though still disconnected,
dangling from a pendulum
one pole to another
seeking synthesis in the middle—
a coming together to deepen and widen
the cradle of the heart, to unencumber
the spirit and psyche.

160

There is an accidental grace in life
that sings on the open plains
where the container is
fathomless with plenty.
Where the horizon is land and sky—
that infinite line of Earth and ether,
a curve we cannot detect,
only imagine with our inner eye.

This is the expansive green,
the least populated landscape
where I am holy, open.
Where I connect to all that is good.
Where I connect to you
after everything else has fallen away. ◆

Rainmaker

What is the desert like in New Mexico?
Is it friendly?
Frail?
Is it fertile for the imagination
for the thirsty soul?
(Think Georgia O'Keefe.)

When, every so often, rain pelts the earth
does dust fly up into vortices
filling your nostrils, making you sneeze?
Or do you watch from the windows
and wish you could run under it
as if it were a waterfall
but you have become afraid of some things
as time has gone on.

What is the desert like in New Mexico?
Is it wishful thinking?
Harsh in the summer sun?
Stifling, a sauna
evaporating
the poetic muse?

Do you watch football in the winter,
holed up inside, or can you still walk
in the settling dusk, blanched by
a mellowed sky?
Do orange clouds descend as the barometer drops
whispering sentiments your lips cannot?

Only your heart can answer these questions I pose
about the desert: Sophia, wisdom of the soul
taking flight, a new day dawns.

Snow falls as I write this
making everything quiet—silent
like the Montana plain,
except for the sound of breaths.

Remember the sky like the sheen
of a winter dove? ◆

What I Remember About Montana
or Conversation with Eternity

The sky opens up to speak.
Through wind and rain it rumbles.
Its refusal to conform to the decorum
of landscape, though noble, is sometimes
rebellious to the point of annoyance.

Sky here scorches the fragrant land
with tongues of fire
wispy clouds, orange bright
like a prism splitting light
in vectors one to the river
one to the hills.

Trees and brush loosen at root
in desert flame
like old bleached bones
waiting to live again.

Then in sudden sweetness of dusk
the rebel firmament lights down
upon our faces calmly, as if medicine.
It speaks not in puzzles, myth or rhyme
but in the etymology of infinity
bearing fruit of future memories.
Ashen seeds of Paintbrush
and Columbine bloom
from our mouths
in silent psalm
under darkening sky.

Dutifully I await an encore
of this fire earth opera.

Especially in Montana
is the sky expansive
across the plain. ◆

What They Saw
for Dryw

I.
The Earth dawned
in Space.
The astronauts pointed their fingers
in awe.
Out of the darkness,
the sun's flares lit up
our oceans and mountains.
Out of the darkness,
the light came
and we became the light.

II.

David R. Scott of Gemini VIII wrote:

> I was in hopes of capturing
> the magnificence of the scene,
> particularly the airglow and thunderheads.

Airglow and thunderheads encircling the Earth at dawn.
What could be more beautiful than this?

How does one get to space nowadays?
Buddhist meditation may be the quickest route.
All that dark space
into which we fall.
A wispy silence
an overwhelming calm.
Yes we have "monkey mind" to contend with
but every thirtieth breath or so
we experience mini-enlightenment:
freedom from the bonds of thought.
We feel released into space
as if orbiting in the Gemini
floating free of gravity
trying to catch packets of food
and wave to our children on video.

III.
What else did they see?
Clouds over the water.
Mostly clouds over the water.

This old red NASA book is poetic.
My favorite line is this:
    Coconut, breadfruit, and pandanus trees
    grow on these remote islands
    and the limpid waters of their lagoons
    yield pearl oysters.

I want to go there
and eat breadfruit
even though I don't know
what that is.

Does wading in lagoons
feel like gel on your calves
until you cut your foot
on an open oyster shell?

IV.
What they saw was this:
autumn, summer and winter
happening simultaneously.
But no people.
They did not see us up close.

They saw the beautiful serene globe
maneuvering around the sun
being lit up by a star ball
the center of all things.

They saw the moon travelling around us.
They saw God through the Earth enfolding us.
They saw that we are
protected by outer gases.
That we are held within the shape.
By the rain, the trees and clouds
we are held.

That is what they saw. ◆

Differences in Air

i. Pacific Northwest Air

musk and pine
organic mulch from
old growth forest stands
moistened bark
steam
there's no inhaling this air
this air you have to swallow

life living and dying
death creating life
all this wild abundance
a green menagerie
made possible
by the shade of only
152 days of sun per year

ii. Sonoran Desert Air

clear and dry
vapor made spare
and dilute by
325 days of sun per year
no humus additives
resting on my tongue
no thick bogginess
for my lungs
to laboriously inhale
no briny water stuck
in the ridges of my throat

Just air
simple, unadorned
easy in easy out
pellucid with a tinge of
hidden nectar
air so weightless
it doesn't feel like breathing at all ◆

seeking to be open, to be free

How do we return to innocence?

That dancing for the sky
brilliant star innocence
blissfully footloose
unaware of grief
like sparkling dew
on butterflies' wings.

How do we become free again
so that the edges of ourselves
bleed into the world around us
leaving no distinction
only one soul
burning in the light?

How do we become so free
that our threadbare hearts
unravel in the wind
releasing prayers
like Sanskrit flags
waving above the graves of olden souls?

Can every breath we exhale
be a blessing to the Earth?

It's not a question; it's a mandate.
It has to happen
or else we will lose everything
that never, ever belonged to us. ◆

X. ARS POETICA

on the ledge of life
saffron dust a mandala
poems whisper yes

Morning Hours

My mind drifts
in the morning
haze
searching
for the muse
to anchor me. ◆

Rebel
for Sally

She was supposed to give them
apple pie.

Instead, she waltzed into
the bright-eyed classroom
steeled herself with grit and righteousness
lifted her head with poise
and gave them
poetry.

Once they realized they were not getting pie
(a few stanzas in)
the boys appeared crestfallen
resentful even—no sugar
to pump through their veins
only the sweet melody
of words to confound them
and elevate them to lofty places.

Poetry to fritter the day away?
thought those solemn spectators
oozing with machismo
their mouths still watering.
No fair!

In their hunger and woe
they rejected what she had to give
and sat cross-armed, steaming.

But the girls—in their rich, ambient imaginations
relished every syllable
emerging from the young poet's mouth.
Every sensuous sound
of burning castles
heartache
searching for their wonderland.
They gobbled up ALL OF IT
as if these words were the last morsels
of beauty to be had.

The boys (so focused on deprivation)
were unaffected by the jewels
she shared.
Their souls didn't open
even an inch.

Or so it appeared.
On the outside.
On the inside they were quivering.

Instead of savoring the apple syrup
that bubbles through the crust,
they feasted surreptitiously
on the rebel act of poetry.
Who was this girl, graceful and
gutsy in her refusal to conform?
How dare she!
They loved it.

A slice of apple pie is so easily forgotten,
but this girl and these words
they would never forget. ◆

The Annoyance of Poetry

She doesn't have access
to the stove anymore.
Been there, done that.
She doesn't remember
what she did yesterday,
what you said five minutes ago,
or if she let the dog
in or out,
but she remembers Keats.
And Shelley.
And Wordsworth.
And cummings.
Poets you used to love
before six months
of ringing repetitiously through the night.
You want to like it,
this constant recitation--
she gets so much joy from it.
If not joy, at least respite.
A pocket of memory
that has not faded
one bit.

What region of the brain
which cluster of cells
harbors poetry
while the tissue surrounding it
falls limp and desiccates?

You never thought poetry
could be annoying.
She may think it's a gift
she's giving you.
By now, however,
it is a madness shared.
Ode on a Grecian Urn
while dressing her.
Every. Single. Morning.
Tintern Abbey while driving
the same scenic route
just to get out of the house.
These well-crafted poems
used to be your favorites.
You relied on them to
elevate your mind and senses.
She wooed you with them
four decades ago:
Her full, beautiful lips
speaking delectable truths.
Your memory of yesterday and today
is intact.

So don't forget the poets
from the turn of our
last century:
Maya Angelou.
And Ondaatje.
And Boland.
And Oliver.
Once a longed-for harmony,
now the wordplay
of these gallant poets gets in the way.
It compromises your ability
to concentrate.
And when you are thinking
and doing for two,
concentration is everything.

Your wife.
Your dear, dear wife.
How many in her
lexicon of poesy?
An impressive number.
You used to be in awe.
20, 30, 50 poems memorized?
Must be.

Seems like the stream
goes on forever
until she begins again
with a dignified gusto
and thunderous breath:

> *A thing of beauty*
> *is a joy forever.*
> *Its loveliness increases*
> *it will never pass*
> *into nothingness…*

Keats. ◆

Poetry Contest

the judges want
slam-style poetry
the kind you can hear
in your mind
rhythm and pulse
deafening

they are looking for
that one poet
the unknown firebrand
who strings words together
mellifluously
as if one potent run-on sentence climaxing with the
epiphany we all need to hear (gasp):

    Don't give up.
    You are loved.
    You sing a chorus of beautiful
                whoever you are.

written clandestinely in
poetic schema
pure covert exemplum

isn't that what poetry does?
connect us?
make us to see our shared sails
in the shock of blue windstorm?

fuck the judges
if they don't get that ◆

Holy Found

The Poet strives above all else
to give shape and memory
to Beauty.
To capture and illuminate
the quiet truths kept hidden
against their will
in our eyes, souls, mouths.
We mistake our bodies
as hesitant, lazy
not realizing that
our physical selves
are eager for a reason
to stretch and yawn
to awaken in celebration
of all that is real and true.

Poetry is a healing endeavor
its honesty jarring
though achingly graceful
crafted by imperfect beings
fumbling in forests of
ashen clear-cut and verdant splendor
frightful risk, sweet empathy.

All we must do
is unknot our scarves
to reveal our hearts
and release the feisty
moistening our lips
so we may conjure the hidden world
for all to see.
In its ideal form
poetry sets both
Poet and reader free—
Free to behold Beauty everywhere.
To be washed clean and holy found
to receive Beauty's pure form
collecting in cupped palms
the real and true of it. ◆

Free

Something about writing
sets me free.
Words are like cells:
what I am made of.
Units full of
spark and spunk.
Electrifying life. ◆

That God-Forsaken Hour

Saturday pre-dawn,
poems elude me.
Their syntax
still sleepy-eyed
at 5:15 AM.

The word-fairies lay dormant, lightless
as I reach for coffee and
my body shakes itself from
slumber's weighty fog.

Soon, however.
Soon the words will jiggle loose
and flow from me like honey
and the night will shed itself
across the cobalt horizon.

A poem is a gift to create
even if the only reader
is the sacred stranger
in a dream carefully ingesting
every word, breath, and sigh.

This early in the morning,
I sit solo with paper
and pen, these scribblings
a secret treasure—
the lone key I will swallow. ◆

What Poetry Becomes

Awe cannot be falsely generated
Thus poetry defies discipline
It may grow into habit
however
when it becomes
an inspired conduit of self
undisputed state of being
undeniable expression
of personality enfleshed
in the context of life
undulating
When it becomes a
stampede of flair
impetuous motion
dictatorial choreography
stasis in art
It cycles through
the interference of
pesky emotions that
cajole a rational person
into disruption, disarray
It becomes you—
this arc of revelation
It needs your spry attitude
your emboldened whimsy
to pinpoint the
firebrand of beauty
not everyone sees ◆

How to Make Sense of Contrast

Poetry is an outlandish rebel
antithetical to life's banality
too flashy to seem real
when situated among
generic acquiescence
and yada yada yada

Poetry defies complacency
delighting with tangy
surprise
Sometimes sizzling
in-your-face
   a marquee on opening night
   flapper dress twirling
   knock-down drag-out

Other times tranquil
nuanced
   a child blissfully asleep
   hot cocoa steaming
   fireflies buzzing in a jar

The Poet strips away
pretense, illusion
distilling life to
rudimentary truth
in tight and pithy form
piquing beauty
beyond propriety
to pure indulgent sense

protesting the ruse
of the American Dream
in favor of a rebel's dream
the holler of King or Che
through sticky mesh
that binds us

Poetry is a strange peg
quizzically out of place
like true love hidden
in rubbish
or lost in war with
limbs askew

How to see the beauty of life
whilst saving it
how to sense a voice, a touch
amongst the ravaged
how to find a gasp of heaven
in all this mess

Hard to synthesize
this magnitude of contrast
this battery of opposites
contentious
across boundaries
a heartbreaking exercise
with impossible stakes
though the Poet dies
trying
hitting the mark
every now and then
when it comes to the
distillation of
love
in particular ◆

Cinder Block

In what life do all clouds
coalesce into one
so we must not guess
at their metamorphosis
but see without mesmery
the genesis, the direction
of life indefinitely
reflected wholly in
the open sky?
How to let go of
wailing and seeking?

Humans seek in vain!
Lost forever in the
dusky gloam of endless tides
pulling us under
to where there is
no being found
ankles tied to
cinder block with
invincible knots.
Everywhere a gangster.
Everywhere a gangster
out to do bad.
No redemption in the heat
for us, no point in trying.
No point.

Poetry redeems.
The moment I stop believing this,
gone will be all my breaths
across time to the
final horizon where,
motioning towards the edge,
I whisper "Fly." ◆

Iridescence

Dead dragonflies
line the sidewalk.
Dozens of them,
a curious sight.
Not artificially placed
just naturally so
and still intact.
They look crisp from
the potent rays of
late afternoon sun
some re-moistened
by cool evening rain.

For humans autumn is
a sweet dormancy.
For these harmless creatures
it is a noble harbinger.

Most lie belly-up prone and dead-looking
although a few have been righted
by the wind.
These latter ones appear alive
and ready for flight.
How tempting it is
to set a finger lightly
upon their wings
nudge them all awake
and watch the rare one
twitch from its cultish
slumber to fly away.

Surely it would not go far;
it would merely hover
over the sidewalk
in search of solitude—
perhaps tuck itself under
a low-hanging bough,
settling in for last rites.

As for its lifeless
brothers and sisters
a finger (no matter how gently laid)
upon their iridescent wings
would not awaken them
but would flake away
the latticework of vein
upon rice paper
leaving small piles
of crumbs at our feet.

The wings of dragonflies
once touched
take on the
consistency of stardust
and form the
circumference of halos.

Some people believe
new life
comes through death. ◆

Reverie

Poems come to me in the dark
when my eyes are healed
when I do not distinguish
my body from the air.
In a dream the poems come.

When I awake the words fall
from my skin and I forget
the misty-eyed soliloquies
I'd composed like Keats
though I remember him.

I always remember John Keats
who led me through the forest
to the Emerald inside the rock
our true love carved in stone.
Holding his hand I traipsed in the wake
of his tousled amber hair.
He wrote odes among the trees for me.

When you believe in reincarnation
anything is possible.
Love can be written
centuries apart. ◆

CPSIA information can be obtained
at www.ICGtesting.com
Printed in the USA
FFHW010935310119
50363523-55460FF